DATE DUE ☑ W9-CTO-475

SAN JOSE UNI

629.13   C. 1
ROS   Rosenblum, Richard $10.95
             The Airplane ABC

EMPIRE GARDENS ELEMENTARY SCHOOL
1060 E. EMPIRE STREET
SAN JOSE, CA. 95112

DEMCO

THE AIRPLANE ABC

Books by Richard Rosenblum

IF GRANDMA HAD WHEELS
Jewish Folk Sayings
(Compiled by Ruby G. Strauss)

THE GOLDEN AGE OF AVIATION

THE AIRPLANE ABC

FOKKER T-2, 1923

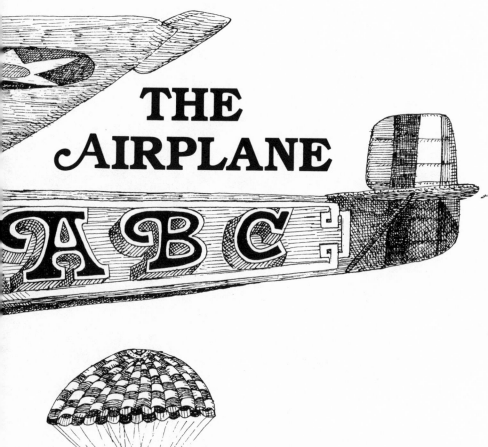

THE
AIRPLANE

ABC

BY RICHARD ROSENBLUM

ATHENEUM 1986 NEW YORK

Library of Congress Cataloging-in-Publication Data

Rosenblum, Richard.   The airplane ABC.

SUMMARY: From amphibians to zeppelins,
presents an alphabet of aircraft and people important
in the history of aviation.
1. Aeronautics—Dictionaries, Juvenile.
[1. Aeronautics—Dictionaries. 2. Alphabet] I. Title.
TL509.R59   1986   629.13′003′21   85-28760
ISBN 0-689-31162-1

Copyright © 1986 by Richard Rosenblum
All rights reserved
Published simultaneously in Canada by
Collier Macmillan Canada, Inc.
Text set by Linoprint Composition, New York City
Printed and bound by Maple-Vail, Binghamton, New York
Typography by Mary Ahern
First Edition

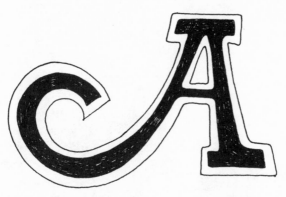

Is for **cAmphibians.**

These airplanes fly from land or sea.

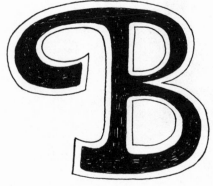 Is for **B**ristol
Bulldog.
An RAF (Royal Air Force) fighter
plane of the late 1920s and early
'30s.

Is for **"Wrong Way"** **Corrigan.**

"Wrong Way" Corrigan
took off for California and
landed in Ireland.

Is for
Dc-3.

The transport plane that made it possible to fly from coast to coast in less than twenty-four hours.

Is for **Amelia Earhart.** She held
many flying records, but she
disappeared during an attempt to
fly around the world.

THE FRIENDSHIP

Is for **The Fokker DR.1.** The three-winged fighter plane of World War I flown by Germany's flying ace, the Red Baron.

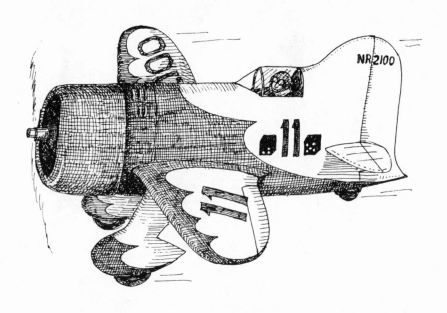

Is for **The GeeBee.** The racing plane piloted by Jimmy Doolittle in the 1929 Thompson Trophy Races.

CURTISS P-6 HAWK
1929

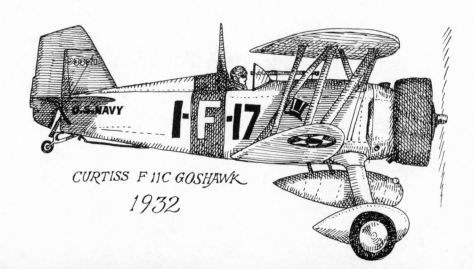

CURTISS F 11C GOSHAWK
1932

Is for **The Curtis Hawks.** All the
Curtis pursuit planes built for the
Army and Navy during the 1920s,
'30s, and '40s.

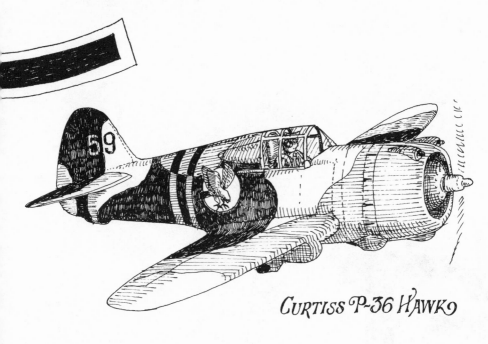

CURTISS P-36 HAWK

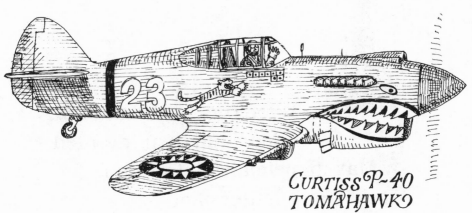

CURTISS P-40
TOMAHAWK

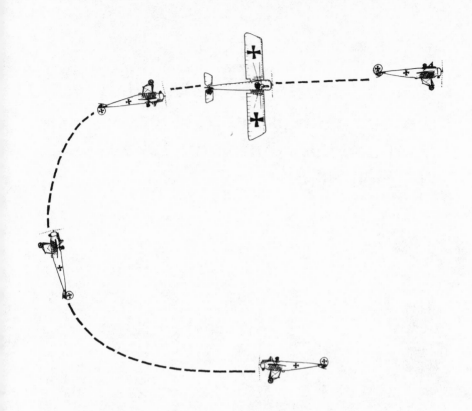

Is for **The Immelmann.**
A loop and turn invented
by Max Immelmann, a German
World War I fighter pilot.

Is for **The Jenny.** A World War I airplane that was later used as a "barnstormer," and air circus plane.

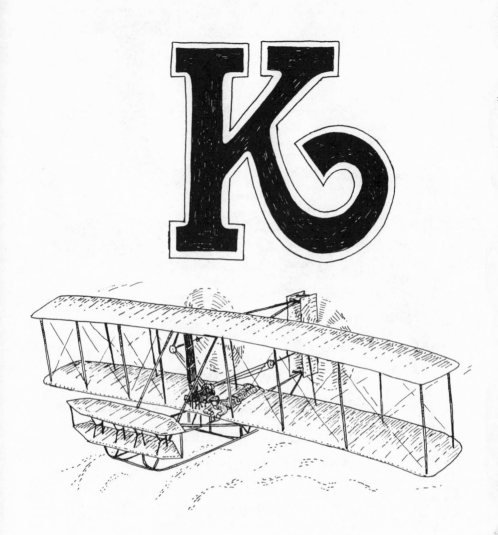

Is for **Kitty Hawk.** This is where the Wright brothers flew their airplane.

THE SPIRIT of ST. LOUIS

L Is for **Lindbergh** the "Lone Eagle." He was the first person to fly alone across the Atlantic Ocean from New York to Paris.

Is for **M**ail **planes.** Fragile planes flown by the hero pilots who pioneered flying the U.S. Mail.

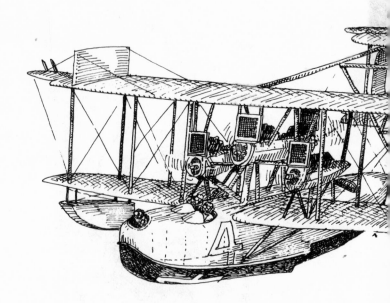

Is for **N**c4. The first airplane to cross the Atlantic Ocean.

Empire Gardens
L.M.C.

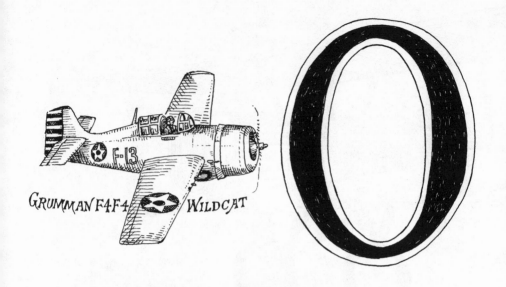

GRUMMAN F4F4 WILDCAT

Is for **"Butch"** 'Hare.
He was the first Navy flying ace of
World War II. O'Hare International
Airport in Chicago is named
after him.

THE
WINNIE MAE

Is for **Wiley** **P**ost.
He flew his airplane, *The Winnie Mae*, around the world on two separate record-breaking flights.

Is for **The Question Mark.** It
stayed aloft for 72 hours in 1929.
There were three future generals in
the crew.

Is for **Eddie Rickenbacker**
World War I flying ace. He was
leader of the Hat-in-the-Ring
Squadron.

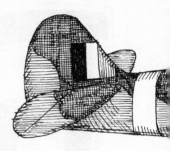

Is for **S**pitfire.
The heroic airplane of the Battle
of Britain, during WWII.

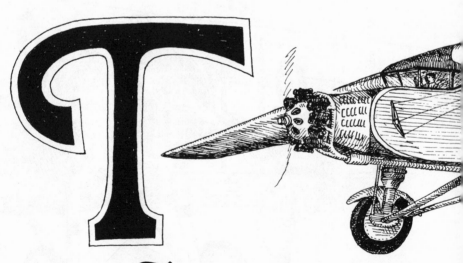

Is for **The** **T**in **Goose.**

The Ford company's famous airliner was born in 1926.

Is for

The **U**-2.

A famous spy
plane of the 1960s.

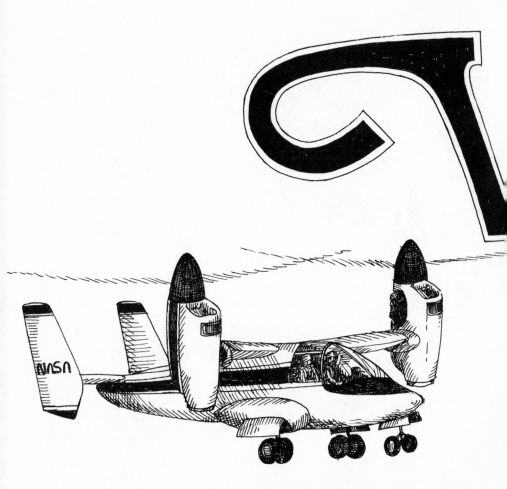

Is for **V**TOL,
vertical take-off and
landing airplane. It lands straight
down and takes off straight up.

Is for **W**AFS, Women's Auxiliary
Ferry Service. They were women
pilots who flew for the Air Corps
during World War II.

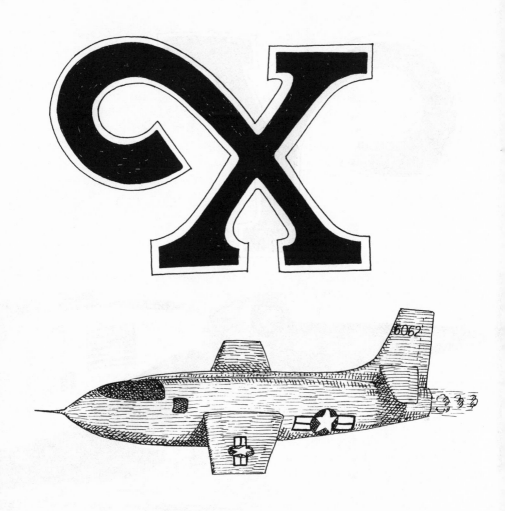

Is for **The** **X**-1. It once was
the fastest plane in the world.

Is for **The Yankee Clipper.**

The plane used in the first American
trans-Atlantic passenger service.

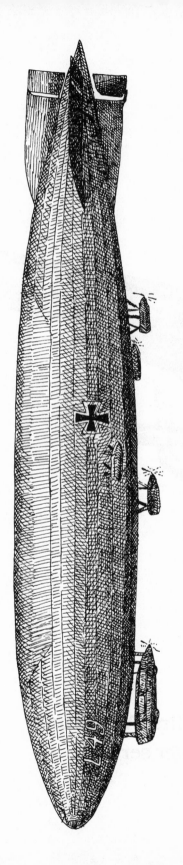

Is for **Z**eppelin.

Count von Zeppelin's lighter-than-air flying machine was a huge airship.

Empire Gardens
L.M.C.